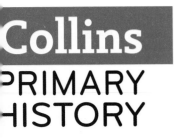

Collins
PRIMARY
HISTORY

Events
Living Memory

Pupil Book

G000019352

Sue Temple | Alf Wilkinson

William Collins' dream of knowledge for all began with the publication of his first book in 1819.
A self-educated mill worker, he not only enriched millions of lives, but also founded a flourishing publishing house. Today, staying true to this spirit, Collins books are packed with inspiration, innovation and practical expertise. They place you at the centre of a world of possibility and give you exactly what you need to explore it.

Collins. Freedom to teach.

Published by Collins
An imprint of HarperCollins*Publishers*
The News Building
1 London Bridge Street
London
SE1 9GF

Browse the complete Collins catalogue at
www.collins.co.uk

© HarperCollins*Publishers* Limited 2019

Maps © Collins Bartholomew 2019

10 9 8 7 6 5 4 3 2 1

ISBN 978-0-00-831079-0

All rights reserved. No part of this publication may be reproduced, stored in a retrieval system, or transmitted in any form by any means, electronic, mechanical, photocopying, recording or otherwise, without the prior written permission of the Publisher or a licence permitting restricted copying in the United Kingdom issued by the Copyright Licensing Agency Ltd, Barnard's Inn, 86 Fetter Lane, London, EC4A 1EN.

British Library Cataloguing-in-Publication Data
A catalogue record for this publication is available from the British Library.

Authors: Sue Temple and Alf Wilkinson
Publisher: Lizzie Catford
Product developer: Natasha Paul
Copyeditor: Sally Clifford
Indexer: Jouve India Private Ltd
Proofreader: Nikky Twyman
Image researcher: Alison Prior
Map designer: Gordon MacGilp
Cover designer and illustrator: Steve Evans
Internal designer: EMC Design
Typesetter: Jouve India Private Ltd
Production controller: Rachel Weaver
Printed and bound by Martins the Printers

MIX
Paper from
responsible sources
FSC™ C007454

This book is produced from independently
certified FSC™ paper to ensure responsible
forest management.

For more information visit:
www.harpercollins.co.uk/green

The publishers gratefully acknowledge the permission granted to reproduce the copyright material in this book. Every effort has been made to trace copyright holders and to obtain their permission for the use of copyright material. The publishers will gladly receive any information enabling them to rectify any error or omission at the first opportunity.

Contents

Introduction

All through history amazing things have happened. Some of these were natural events, like volcanoes or floods. Others were caused by people, like starting a fire, or someone making a discovery by accident or by their hard work. By reading about the events in this book you will learn about just a few of these amazing historical events, which happened all around the world.

When we talk about these events, we use the word 'significant'. This means the event was something that is interesting and important. However, everyone has different ideas about what should be called 'significant'. You may know about events in your own town or local area, which you feel are important and interesting. You could look at the following reasons to help you decide if the event you are thinking about should be called 'significant'.

Reasons for an event being significant

If it:

- changed events at the time it happened.
- improved lots of people's lives – or made them worse.
- changed people's ideas.
- had a long-lasting impact on its country or the world.
- was a very good example, or a very bad example, of something.

Adapted from Dawson 2017

We hope this book will help you to learn about a few different events you may not have heard about before. We think they are significant – but you might not agree. Have fun!

Timeline of events

79 Mount Vesuvius erupts

0   100   200   300   400   500   600   700

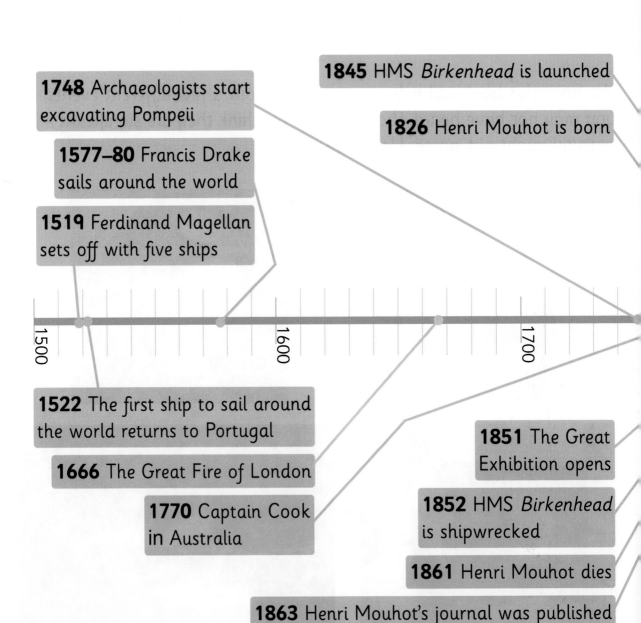

1845 HMS *Birkenhead* is launched

1748 Archaeologists start excavating Pompeii

1826 Henri Mouhot is born

1577–80 Francis Drake sails around the world

1519 Ferdinand Magellan sets off with five ships

1500   1600   1700

1522 The first ship to sail around the world returns to Portugal

1666 The Great Fire of London

1770 Captain Cook in Australia

1851 The Great Exhibition opens

1852 HMS *Birkenhead* is shipwrecked

1861 Henri Mouhot dies

1863 Henri Mouhot's journal was published

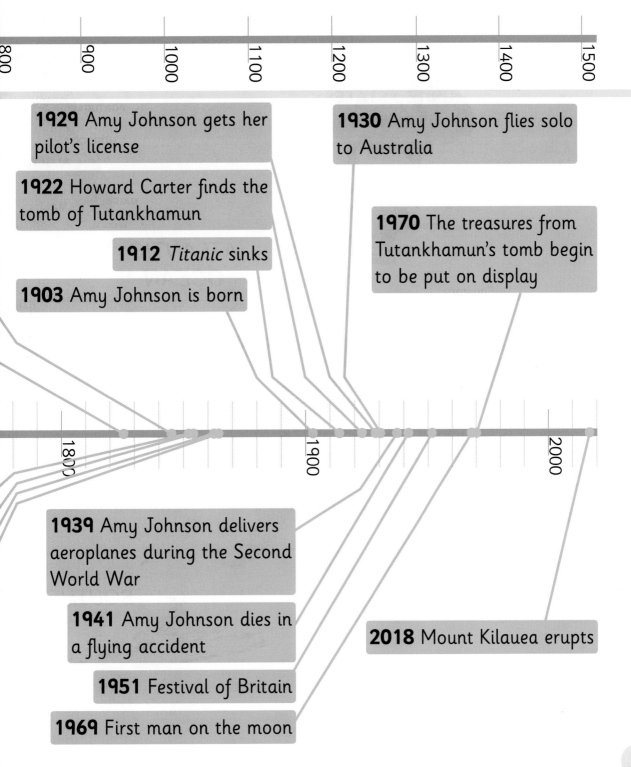

800
900
1000
1100
1200
1300
1400
1500

1929 Amy Johnson gets her pilot's license

1930 Amy Johnson flies solo to Australia

1922 Howard Carter finds the tomb of Tutankhamun

1970 The treasures from Tutankhamun's tomb begin to be put on display

1912 *Titanic* sinks

1903 Amy Johnson is born

1800
1900
2000

1939 Amy Johnson delivers aeroplanes during the Second World War

1941 Amy Johnson dies in a flying accident

2018 Mount Kilauea erupts

1951 Festival of Britain

1969 First man on the moon

7

World map

North Pole +

GREENLAND

ICELAND   NORWAY   SW

CANADA

UNITED
KINGDOM DENMAR
IRELAND
GERMA
AUS
FRANCE   CRO
PORTUGAL   SPAIN   ITA

UNITED STATES
OF AMERICA

MOROCCO
ALGERIA

MEXICO

MAURITANIA   MALI   NIGER

CUBA

SENEGAL
JAMAICA
GUINEA
GUATEMALA
NICARAGUA
NIGERIA
COSTA RICA
VENEZUELA   GHANA
PANAMA
COLOMBIA   GUYANA

ATLANTIC
OCEAN

Equator
ECUADOR   GABON

PERU   BRAZIL

PACIFIC
OCEAN
BOLIVIA
NA

PARAGUAY
CHILE

URUGUAY
ARGENTINA

SOUTHERN O

South Pole +

ARCTIC OCEAN

RUSSIA

KAZAKHSTAN

MONGOLIA

NE

TURKEY

TURKMENISTAN

SYRIA

AFGHANISTAN

AEL

IRAQ

IRAN

JORDAN

PT

SAUDI
ARABIA

PAKISTAN

NEPAL

CHINA

JAPAN

PACIFIC
OCEAN

OMAN

INDIA

MYANMAR

DAN

ERITREA YEMEN

THAILAND

PHILIPPINES

VIETNAM

UTH
DAN

ETHIOPIA

SRI
LANKA

SOMALIA

MALAYSIA

KENYA

Equator

TANZANIA

INDIAN
OCEAN

INDONESIA

PAPUA NEW
GUINEA

MOZAMBIQUE

SOLOMON
ISLANDS

MADAGASCAR

VANUATU

AUSTRALIA

NEW
ZEALAND

Mount Vesuvius and Pompeii

▲
Ruins of Pompeii, Italy

What happened?

Pompeii, Italy, 79 CE

At 1 p.m. on 22 August 79 CE, Mount Vesuvius in Italy **erupted.** Ash, **pumice stone** and gas were thrown 33 kilometres into the air. **Lava** rushed down the hillside, covering everything in its path. Over 1500 people died. Historians think that many more probably died, but their bodies have never been discovered.

Erupted:
This is when a volcano explodes, throwing out hot gases, stones and lava.

Pumice stone:
This is a volcanic rock, usually light-coloured.

Lava:
This is the hot liquid which pours out of the top of a volcano.

Luckily, we have an eye witness account of events. Pliny the Younger lived nearby. This is what he said:

"Ashes were falling, not as yet very thickly. I looked round: a **dense black cloud** was coming up behind us, spreading over the earth like a flood... darkness fell, not the dark of a moonless or cloudy night, but as if the lamp had been put out in a closed room. You could hear the shrieks of people..."

Dense black cloud: Thick, dark cloud which is difficult to see through.

Mount Vesuvius erupts

Danger

As soon as Vesuvius began to erupt, many of the people in Pompeii fled, but many more decided to stay in their own homes, where they thought they would be safe. Within a few hours, Pompeii was covered with a 3-metre layer of rocks and ash. Many people were killed when the roof of their house collapsed on top of them because of the weight of rocks and ash. Some were killed in the street, trying to run away.

Most people were killed by either the heat or the hot gases — archaeologists think it was at least 300 degrees Centigrade. Herculaneum, another nearby town, was buried under 23 metres of lava and ash! More lava completely covered Pompeii, hiding any evidence that there had ever been a town there at all.

Mount Kilauea, Hawaii, 2018

Volcanoes are still erupting — on 3 May 2018, Mount Kilauea erupted. Ash, smoke and gas were thrown up to 6000 metres into the air above Hawaii. The ash cloud covered an area of 31 square kilometres. Nearly 600 houses were destroyed, and over 2000 people had to be evacuated from their homes. Nearly 100 metres were blown off the top of the mountain. Luckily, no one was killed or injured in the eruption.

Mount Kilauea erupting

Mount Vesuvius and Pompeii

What was life like then?

Pompeii was a busy town of around 20,000 people, built on the slopes of Mount Vesuvius. Previous eruptions had made the soil around Vesuvius very rich, and lots of crops grew there. Naples was only 9 kilometres away. It was a good place to live.

There had been an earthquake in the area in 62 CE and there was lots of evidence of the people rebuilding the town. There was a trench down the middle of one street, where a water pipe was being replaced.

What happened next?

Nobody lived in Pompeii again after 79 CE. There is evidence that people later dug tunnels into the lava to steal valuable items. But Pompeii remains a complete Roman town. The eruption happened so quickly that most people were not able to escape, so they remained, like their houses, buried under the lava. Archaeologists have found bread that had been

An excavated street in Pompeii
▼

baking in the oven. In another house, a meal was still on the table. Wall paintings show people going about their everyday business.

Archaeologists in Pompeii

How do we know what happened?

As we have already seen, Pliny the Younger wrote about the destruction of Pompeii. Also, since 1748, archaeologists have slowly excavated the town, although much still remains to be uncovered. Only recently, in February 2018, archaeologists found the skeleton of a child who had tried to hide in the public baths. He or she had been killed by the poisonous gases from the volcano.

Slowly, surely, Pompeii is giving up its secrets. It is the best-preserved Roman town anywhere in the world. It gives us a snapshot of life in a Roman town in 79 CE, which is about the time the Romans were settling in Britain. And it reminds us how dangerous nature can be!

Let's think about it!

Compare the Pompeii eruption with a more recent one, such as Mount Kilauea. What is the same? What is different?

Find out about the work of archaeologists. What do they do and how do they work out what has happened in each site they explore?

Find out what happens when a volcano erupts.

2.1 Discovering Angkor Wat

What happened?

A grave in the middle of nowhere

In the jungle near the town of Luang Prabang in Laos, Southeast Asia, is a grave. A Frenchman, Henri Mouhot, was buried there in 1861. He died of malaria. A simple stone was erected in 1867 but it was washed away by floods. This monument was put up in 1887. What was Henri doing so far away from home?

The tomb of Henri Mouhot

Henri Mouhot

Henri was born in a small town in the south of France in 1826. He spent 10 years in Russia before moving to England in 1857 to get married. He married the daughter of Mungo Park, a Scot who explored West Africa.

Henri was a naturalist – someone who studied plants and animals. He read a book, *The People and Kingdom of Siam*, and decided he must go there. He tried to get money and help from the French government but they refused. Finally, the Royal Geographical Society and the Zoological Society in London supported him. They wanted him to send them new plants and animals for their collections. He set off for Thailand in 1858.

In the jungle

Henri made four journeys into the jungles of Laos, Cambodia and Thailand before he died. He kept lots of notes and a detailed diary. He sometimes sketched what he found. He sent letters home, discussing his discoveries. He also sent his supporters in London some examples of the animals, plants and shells he discovered. Most of the time, he was the only European for kilometres around. When he died, one of his servants took all his papers to the coast and they were sent home to his wife.

Henri Mouhot and his two servants in the jungle – a drawing based on one of his sketches, published in London in 1864

What was life like then?

Angkor

Angkor been the capital city of the **Khmer** Empire from around 1000 CE to around 1400 CE. The Khmers had ruled Vietnam, Laos, Thailand and Myanmar (also known as Burma). They were very rich and powerful. One or two Europeans had been there before, but not many. Most people did not travel to other countries then, especially not to far away countries like Thailand.

> **Khmer:**
> This is a group of people who lived in Cambodia a long time ago, around 1000 CE. Their language is still spoken by many people in Southeast Asia.

The city of Angkor – or what was left of it – covered 390 square kilometres, but it was in ruins. Wooden houses and palaces had rotted away. There were ancient terraces, pools, palaces and temples. Most were covered in jungle creepers and giant trees. It had been a very rich city. But why had it been abandoned? Henri found Angkor Wat in January 1860, but he didn't find out who had built it or why. If Henri had not described Angkor Wat in his writing, people in Europe might not have known about it for many years.

Angkor Wat

Angkor Wat is a giant temple. It is still the biggest religious site in the world. Henri wrote about how huge it was, even after it had been deserted for 400 or 500 years. He thought it was as impressive as the Egyptian Pyramids or the ruins of Rome. However, he didn't think that the Khmers could have built it. He said that it must have been other people before them.

Part of Angkor Wat, sketched by Henri Mouhot

Discovering Angkor Wat

What happened next?

Making Angkor famous

After Henri died in 1861, his journal was published in 1863. It made lots of people very interested in Cambodia and Laos. Tourists began to visit the area. Today, 2 million people visit Angkor Wat every year! Archaeologists began to excavate the ruins.

Every year, two million people visit this palace

Finding out more

Slowly, over time, we have learned a lot more about Angkor and the Khmer people. We now know that Henri was wrong, that Angkor *was* built by the Khmers and that many of the temples were covered in gold and precious stones. We also know that during the Middle Ages (when Henry VIII was King of England) there was a large rich and powerful country covering a huge area of what is now Cambodia and much of Vietnam, Laos, Thailand and Myanmar. However very few people outside the city knew about it. It is all because a young Frenchman decided to go off and explore Thailand that we now know so much about it.

▲ *Portrait of Henri Mouhot*

Let's think about it!

This story shows that sometimes historians get it wrong. Unless you have all the evidence, you can get the wrong idea. What kinds of evidence do historians use to make their decisions?

Why did Henri think this site was as important as the Egyptian Pyramids or Roman ruins? Do you agree with him?

Find out more about this ancient city and why it was abandoned.

What happened?

Explorers

By 1519, Portuguese sailors had been exploring Africa and India for years. In 1497, Vasco da Gama sailed around the coast of Africa and reached India. He brought back lots of spices, which were very valuable. In 1505, a young Portuguese sailor, Ferdinand Magellan, joined a fleet of ships sailing to Malacca in the Spice Islands. During the trip he acquired a slave called Enrique. Ferdinand returned to Portugal in 1511 as a very rich man.

Ferdinand Magellan was captain of the expedition

Around the world

Magellan tried to persuade the king of Portugal to pay for him to sail to the Spice Islands via the Atlantic Ocean, the way Christopher Columbus had sailed in 1492. When the king refused, Magellan moved to Spain instead. In 1519, the king of Spain paid for Magellan, a fleet of five ships and 237 men to go to the Spice Islands and bring back **cloves**.

Cloves:
These are the flower buds of a tree grown in Indonesia. They are used in cooking to flavour dishes, or to make things smell nice.

Magellan's ships

23

3.2 Sailing round the world

The voyage

On 20 September 1519, Magellan and his five ships left Seville, in Spain on what was to become the first ever round-the-world voyage. He crossed the Atlantic and landed in Brazil to take on fresh food and water, then headed south to Patagonia. He reported that 3-metre-tall giants lived there! He lost one of his ships there, before sailing around the tip of South America – the first European to do so. He reached the Pacific Ocean, which he called the 'Peaceful Ocean'. It took him a month to sail through what we now know as the Magellan Straits, where another ship was lost. He was the first European to sail in the Pacific Ocean too.

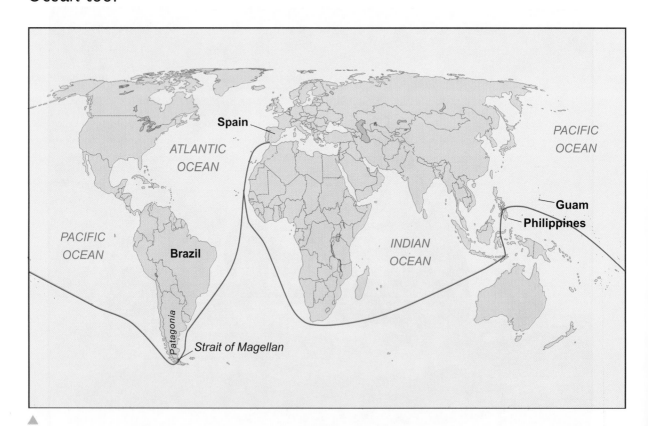

Map showing Magellan's voyage around the world

In the Pacific

The fleet sailed north to Guam and then also became the first Europeans to reach the Philippines. Here, in a fight with natives, Magellan was killed. His body was never found. After the fight, there were only enough sailors to crew two ships, so one was burned and left behind.

The rest of the men sailed for home, stopping off in 1521 in the Spice Islands, where they loaded the two remaining ships with cloves. When they reached Portugal again in 1522, only 18 of the crew who started out together were still alive.

What was life like then?

Spice

A long time ago, in the Middle Ages, it was very difficult to keep food fresh. There were no tins, no fridges or freezers. Food went bad very quickly. They did not have many of the foods we eat now.

One way to make your food taste better was to use lots of spices in cooking – cloves, cinnamon, nutmeg and black pepper. These came from far away and were very expensive.

Spices were used to make the food taste better

3.3 Sailing round the world

What happened next?

Profit

Magellan's voyage made a profit. The 381 sacks of cloves they brought back were worth more than the five ships and 237 men put together! The king of Spain was very pleased and paid for more voyages.

▲ *Bags of cloves were worth a lot of money*

Knowledge

As a result of the voyage, people knew a lot more about the world. Before 1522, the Pacific Ocean was not really known to Europeans. New lands were explored. New sailing routes could be used. People began to realise just how big the world was.

Exploration

The voyage was the first time that anyone had sailed completely around the world. We remember Magellan as the first person to sail around the world because he was the captain of the expedition, but he died in the Philippines in the middle of the Pacific Ocean. Perhaps we should remember instead his slave Enrique as the first person to sail around the world?

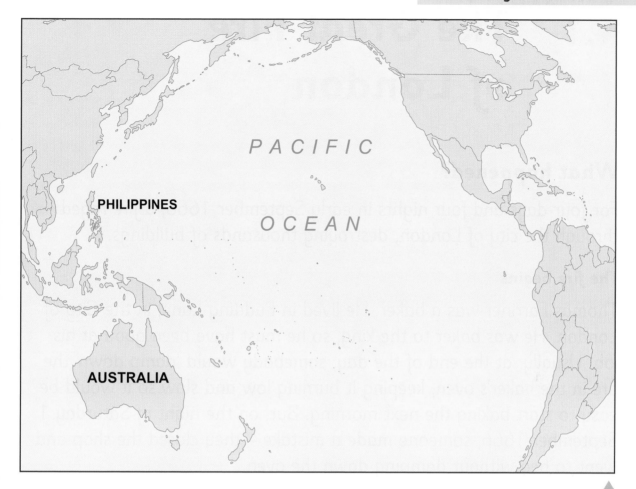

The Pacific Ocean

Exciting others

Other countries and other sailors followed Magellan's example. Between 1577 and 1580, Francis Drake became the first Englishman to sail around the world. Captain Cook was sent to explore the Pacific Ocean and explored Australia in 1770. Suddenly, our picture of the world changed, thanks to brave men like Magellan.

Let's think about it!

Find out which foods you could eat in the Middle Ages. Try tasting some of the spices!

How do we know about these voyages? What evidence do we have?

Find out about other brave explorers, like Ibn Battuta, Christopher Columbus, Neil Armstrong and Mary Kingsley.

The Great Fire of London

What happened?

For four days and four nights in early September 1666, a fire raged through the city of London, destroying thousands of buildings.

The fire begins

Thomas Farriner was a baker. He lived in Pudding Lane, in the City of London. He was baker to the king, so he must have been good at his job! Usually, at the end of the day, somebody would 'damp down' the fire in the baker's oven, keeping it burning low and slow so it would be easy to start baking the next morning. But, on the night of Saturday 1 September 1666, someone made a mistake — they closed the shop and went to bed without damping down the oven.

A painting of London on fire

Disaster

Sparks from the baker's oven set fire to a nearby pile of wood. By 3a.m., huge flames spread through the bakery and the house. Strong winds helped the flames jump from house to house. Soon the fire raced towards the Thames, where warehouses held things like oil. This made the fire worse. It quickly became out of control. London was on fire.

◁ *Escaping the fire*

Fighting the fire

People filled leather buckets with water to try to put out the flames. Houses were pulled down to try to make barriers to stop the fire spreading. Eventually gunpowder was used to blow up houses, but with little success. People fled the city, carrying as many of their possessions as they could. They set up tents and huts to the north of the city, in Islington and Highgate. All they could do was wait for the wind to drop and the fire to die down.

▲ *Leather bucket like those used to fight the fire*

What was life like then?

London in 1666

London was one of the largest cities in the world at the time, with a population of around 500,000. It was a city in shock. Only the year before, the Plague had killed around 100,000 people in London. Samuel Pepys, the famous diarist, had said how strange it was to see the streets so empty.

Fighting a fire in the 17th century

In the 17th century, it is said you could smell a town or city long before you could see it, and London was no exception! The city was covered in smoke and soot, as every house needed a wood or coal fire to keep warm and to cook.

Living in London

500,000 people needed a lot of food. Cows and sheep were walked through the streets to market, then they would be slaughtered and the leftovers chucked in the river. There would be dung everywhere, from the horses that pulled the carts and coaches. There were no sewers or anyone to collect the rubbish, and it had been a hot and dry summer. The River Thames was very low. Houses were really close together and overcrowded. They were mostly made of wood and **thatch**.

Thatch:
This is what some roofs are made of – bundles of dried reeds or straw.

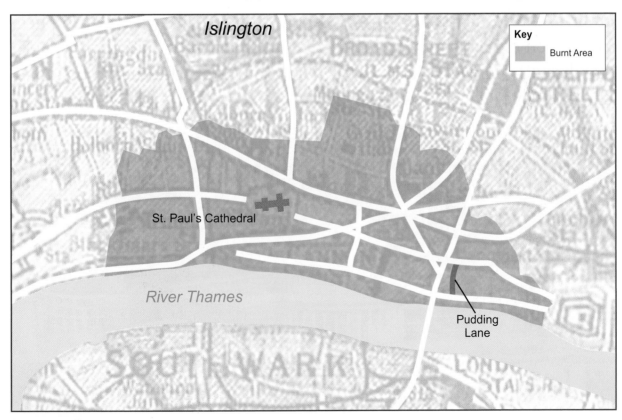

A map of London showing how much of the city was affected

The Great Fire of London

What happened next?

After the fire

By the time the fire burned itself out, over 13,000 houses (90 per cent of those in the city) had been destroyed. 400 streets had been burned down, and 87 churches. Officially, only 6 people died, but it is quite likely that there were many more deaths. We will never know for sure.

Rebuilding

King Charles II was determined that the city would be rebuilt in a safer way. In 1667, new rules for building were introduced. Houses had to be made of stone or brick and placed further apart to prevent the spread of fires. It took nearly 30 years to rebuild London. In 1669, Christopher Wren won a competition to rebuild St Paul's Cathedral, although it took another 40 years to build it. In all, Wren rebuilt 52 churches in London, some of which can still be seen today.

St Paul's Cathedral today

A new fire service

New rules were brought in to fight fires. Each district in the city had to have better firefighting equipment – leather buckets, fire hooks and hand squirts, for example.

A 17th-century fire engine
▼

Let's think about it!

What would you want to save if your home was on fire? How do we know about this fire? Find out about Samuel Pepys and what he saved.

Draw a picture of some of the 17th-century houses. Label your picture with the changes that were made to keep cities safer after the Great Fire.

Why did the fire spread so quickly?

5.1 HMS *Birkenhead*: Women and children first!

What happened?

Have you ever wondered what happens when a ship carrying hundreds of people crashes into something? How is everyone rescued — especially if this occurs in the middle of the Atlantic Ocean? Until the middle of the **20th century**, ships did not have to carry enough lifeboats for everyone on board to be saved. And, if there are not enough lifeboats for everyone, who should be saved?

20th century:
A century is 100 years and the 20th century is the era from 1901 to 2000.

The Wreck of the Birkenhead *— a painting from 1901*

HMS *Birkenhead* was a steamship, built in 1845 for the navy. It was made of iron, so it would not rot like wooden ships did, and had paddle wheels as well as sails. It was quite fast: in 1850, it made the journey from England to Cape Town in South Africa in just 37 days. It was used as a troop ship, taking soldiers and equipment to the British army in South Africa.

HMS:
All ships in the navy had this in their names – it stands for His/Her Majesty's Ship'.

The Final Journey of HMS *Birkenhead*

In January 1852, HMS *Birkenhead* set out from Portsmouth for Cape Town. It carried soldiers, gold to pay the army, and also a small number of officers' wives and children. After picking up more troops in Ireland, the ship reached Cape Town on 23 February. Some soldiers left the ship here, but more women and children joined, as well as nine replacement horses. About 640 men, women and children (no one is sure exactly how many) sailed for Algoa Bay on 25 February.

Danger Point lighthouse in Cape Town, where
HMS Birkenhead *was heading*

5.2 HMS *Birkenhead*: Women and children first!

Rocks!

About 2 a.m. on 26 February, HMS *Birkenhead* hit rocks, ripping a hole in the hull. About 100 men died instantly, killed as the water flooded in below decks. The captain tried to reverse his ship off the rocks, but just made the hole bigger. It was obvious that the ship would sink! It was 3 kilometres off the coast.

HMS Birkenhead *went to the bottom of the sea very quickly. An engraving from 1852*

Abandon ship!

The captain quickly gave the order to abandon ship. The horses were pushed overboard to swim ashore. Only three lifeboats could be lowered. Lieutenant-Colonel Seton, the chief army officer on board, gave the order to his soldiers to stay put. They were to assemble on the deck and help the women and children into the boats. Despite the ship sinking within 25 minutes, all three boats, loaded with women, children and a few sailors to look after them, were launched. The rest of the soldiers stood, as if on parade, on the deck and waited for orders.

A painting from 1892 by Thomas Hemy showing the sinking of the Birkenhead. *A copy of this picture was on the walls of many Victorian classrooms*

Survival

All the women and children safely reached shore. In total, 193 people from the ship were saved. 60 managed to swim 3 kilometres to the shore, although many who tried were eaten by sharks. 40 were rescued from the ship, still clinging to the **rigging,** when help arrived later that day. Eight horses managed to swim ashore. Everyone one else on the ship, including the captain, drowned.

Rigging:
These are the ropes, cables and chains supporting the ship's wooden mast, which holds the sails up.

37

What was life like then?

Travelling by sea

Lots of richer people travelled in Victorian times. They often travelled for pleasure, visiting friends and family. Other people travelled for work or business, or to explore the world. Thousands moved to another country, like Australia Canada or India, to live. Britain had the biggest **empire** in the world at the time and needed people to help run it. People always seemed to be travelling!

Empire:
These are the countries controlled by one other main country.

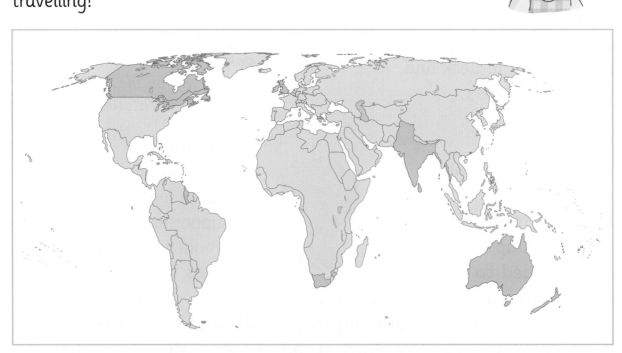

The British Empire in the 1850s – all the countries coloured red were ruled by Britain

What happened next?

Women and children first!

All the women and children on HMS *Birkenhead* were saved, because Lieutenant-Colonel Seton insisted the men give up their places in the lifeboats for all the women and children. As far as we know, it is the first time this happened. Ever since then, when disaster happens, people try to insist on helping women and children first.

A memorial to those from Suffolk who died on HMS Birkenhead *in St Mary's Church, Bury St Edmunds* ▶

Let's think about it!

How realistic are the paintings of the shipwreck? It was 2 a.m., and everything happened so quickly. Would everyone be dressed in uniform? What else might not be accurate?

How do we know what happened? What sources are available?

Find out about travelling by ship. At this time in history, there were no aeroplanes, so you had to go on a ship to get to faraway countries. Find out what it was like to travel on a ship like this.

When the *Titanic* sank in 1912, the idea of 'women and children first' was well established. Were there any other things that were the same or different between the *Titanic* and the *Birkenhead*?

Are there any memorials near your school? Find out why they are there.

6.1 The Crystal Palace

What happened?

The Crystal Palace, as it became known, was built of iron and glass. It was built to hold the Great Exhibition in 1851. It used 300,000 sheets of glass and it took over 5000 workmen to put it together. It was 562 metres long and 124 metres wide. Also, because the builders were not allowed to chop down one of the trees on the site, the Crystal Palace had to be built around it!

A competition was held to design the building. There were 248 entries, but the judges didn't like any of them. In the end, Joseph Paxton was asked to build a hall like one of the greenhouses he had built at Chatsworth House in Derbyshire.

The Crystal Palace was built in 1851

Inside the Great Exhibition

The Great Exhibition

The Great Exhibition opened on 1 May 1851. On opening day, it cost £1 to get in. After that, it cost 5 shillings (25p) until 22 May, then only 1 shilling (5p) on most days, which meant that ordinary people could afford to visit. One old lady walked all the way from Penzance in Cornwall to London to visit the exhibition! By the time it closed, more than 6 million people had visited.

In 1851, for the first time ever, more people lived in towns than in the countryside, and more people worked in industry than in farming. Times were changing, and changing fast. Some people thought it would be a good idea to show off Britain's new industries and products, so the idea to hold the Great Exhibition was born. Prince Albert, Queen Victoria's husband, was one of the main people supporting the idea. It was probably him, more than anyone else, that made the Great Exhibition happen. It was opened by Queen Victoria.

The Crystal Palace

On show

There were over 100,000 items to see in the Great Exhibition. Half were from Britain, and the rest were from all the countries of the world. You could see new inventions and strange foods – there was even a folding piano for sailors! There were also flush toilets for visitors to use.

◀ *These were some of the things on display at the Great Exhibition*

What was life like then?

The 'Workshop of the World'

In 1851 Britain was known as the 'Workshop of the World'. If you wanted to buy wool or cotton cloth, pottery, iron, railways, ships or coal, or many other things, most people around the world bought them from Britain. This made Britain, and some of the people in it, very rich indeed! Factories and workshops seemed to be everywhere, some of them employing thousands of people – men, women and children. People worked very long hours for low wages. For most people, it was difficult to make ends meet.

Thomas Cook organised special trains from around the country to London, so that ordinary people could visit the Great Exhibition.

Many children worked in factories in the Victorian era

What happened next?

After the exhibition

By the time it closed, the Great Exhibition had made a profit. This money was used to buy land and build museums in South Kensington that are still visited today by people from around the world. The organisers also built the Royal Albert Hall. The Crystal Palace was taken down – it was always designed as a temporary building – and moved to a new site in South London. It was still used until it burned down in 1936.

The Victoria and Albert Museum was built to display some of the items from the Great Exhibition

The impact of the exhibition

The Great Exhibition had been designed to show off Britain's wealth and industries to the rest of the world. Unfortunately, it was the exhibits from other countries that people noticed most – new farming machinery from Canada and the United States, and watches from Switzerland. The newspapers featured exotic items from India, China, South America and Australia that people had never seen before. For the first time, millions of people moved easily and cheaply around the country and saw things from all around the world. Britain would never be the same again!

An illustration of the front and back of a watch from Switzerland that was exhibited at the Great Exhibition

Let's think about it!

Why did Prince Albert want to hold this exhibition?

Why did so many people visit it?

Find out about the Victorian inventions which were on display at this exhibition – for example, early version of bicycles and motor cars, printing presses, early versions of hearing loops for the hard of hearing and ink that be understood by touch (Braille) for the blind.

Ask your parents and grandparents which inventions have improved their lives the most.

Find out about the Festival of Britain in 1951.

What happened?

Howard Carter had spent most of his adult life working as an archaeologist in Egypt, looking for Ancient Egyptian treasures. Since 1915, he had been paid by a rich Englishman, Lord Carnarvon, to find and explore Egyptian ruins. On 22 November 1922, Carter smashed a hole in the entrance to a tomb in the Valley of the Kings, near Luxor. As he shone a torch through the hole, he realised that at last he had discovered something really special. He quickly blocked up the hole and sent a message to Lord Carnarvon, who was at home in England. Carter told him to come to Egypt very, very quickly.

River Nile

Valley of the Kings

▲ *Map showing the location of Tutankhamun's tomb in Egypt*

◄ *Howard Carter found the tomb of Tutankhamun*

Entering the tomb

On 17 February 1923, Carter and Carnarvon entered the tomb, and were amazed at what they discovered. It was very unusual. It was the tomb of a **pharaoh** that had not been robbed. It was very small – the smallest in the Valley of the Kings. There were 5389 different items in the tomb. It took Carter 10 years just to make a record of each item. Today, you can see them all in a museum in Cairo, Egypt.

Pharaoh: An Egyptian ruler.

Some of the treasures found in the tomb

What was life like then?

Tutankhamun's treasures

It was the tomb of Tutankhamun, who ruled Egypt around 1300 BCE. He was only 18 years old when he died. He was buried inside three gold coffins, and these were  put inside an extra coffin made of stone. Next to his body was a huge fan made from ostrich feathers. Only pharaohs were allowed to hunt ostriches. There were also musical instruments, beds, chariots and utensils – everything Tutankhamun might need in the **afterlife**.

Afterlife:
This was where the Ancient Egyptians believed you went when you died.

Inside the young pharaoh's tomb

Tutankhamun wore sandals on his feet. Each sole was painted with the face of one of his enemies, so every time he walked he crushed his enemies beneath his feet. Despite all the gold and precious metals, perhaps the most valuable item was a knife made from iron. The Ancient Egyptians didn't have a source of iron. The dagger was made from a **meteorite** that must have landed in the desert.

Meteorite:
A solid piece of rock which has come from outer space.

Nubians:
A group of people who lived in southern Egypt.

Why is Tutankhamun's tomb so important?

Tutankhamun was not very important when he ruled Egypt, and he didn't rule for long. He was very young when he became pharaoh and died aged 18. However, he ruled Egypt when it was a great power, defeating the **Nubians** and keeping Egypt strong.

Tutankhamun's death

Historians are not sure why Tutankhamun died. Some say it was leading his army in battle in Syria. Others think he died in an accident, while hunting ostriches or riding in his chariot. Some say he died of illness. Tutankhamun had a bad leg ('club foot') and walked with a stick, and the latest tests show he may have had epilepsy. As new tests are introduced, we may become nearer to a decision that everyone agrees with!

A recreation of what Tutankhamun might have
◄ *looked like*

What happened next?

The discovery of this tomb has given archaeologists evidence about the items used and made at the time. This has helped us to learn much more about the Ancient Egyptians and how they might have lived.

Tutankhamun and his wife
◄ Ankhsenamun

The 'Curse of the Pharaohs'

A few months after opening the tomb, Lord Carnarvon caught the flu and died. Several other people involved in finding and opening Tutankhamun's tomb died soon after. People began to talk about the 'Curse of the Pharaohs'.

The world goes crazy about Egypt

Discovering the tomb was big news all around the world. It seemed that everyone went 'Egypt crazy'! Women wore Egyptian-style dresses, pop songs were written about Egypt and 'King Tut', as he was known. Howard Carter became famous, touring the world, and especially America, giving lectures about his amazing discovery. Everyone wanted Egyptian things to put in their museums and country houses. Since the 1970s, many of the treasures from the tomb have toured the world, and millions of people have been to see them. There is even a replica of every item found in the tomb in Dorchester, England!

Egyptian-style buildings, like the Carlton Cinema, started appearing across London after Tutankhamun's tomb was found

Let's think about it!

Why do historians argue about how Tutankhamun died? Why don't we know?

Find out more about the treasures found in his tomb. What do they tell us about what people believed then?

Amy Johnson flies to Australia

What happened?

Arriving in Australia

On 24 May 1930, a second hand Gypsy Moth plane, with an open **cockpit**, landed in Darwin, Australia. The pilot, Amy Johnson, was the first woman to fly **solo** from Britain to Australia, a distance of 17,700 kilometres. It took her 19 days. She instantly became one of the most famous women in the world!

Cockpit: Where the pilot sits in a small plane.

Solo: When you do something on your own.

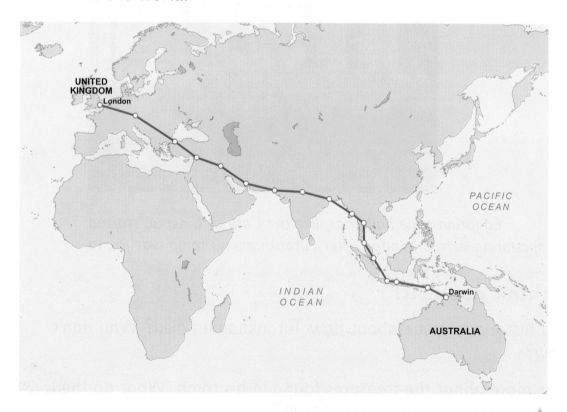

Amy's route from London to Australia

Amy's story

Amy was born in Hull, in 1903, the year the first aeroplane flew. She went to university in Sheffield, before moving to London to work. There, in 1928, she took flying lessons and got her pilot's licence in 1929. She persuaded her father to buy her a second hand aeroplane. In 1929, she was the first woman in the world to get an engineer's licence. All Amy wanted to do was to fly.

Satellite navigation systems:
Helps drivers of all kinds of transport find their way around. They use information from space to know where you are.

Flying to Australia

Amy's journey had to be carefully planned. There were no **satellite navigation systems**, reliable weather reports, or even a radio to talk to people on the ground. Each stop was carefully planned, with fuel and supplies waiting ready for her. The newspapers nicknamed her 'Lone Girl Flyer'. You can see her plane in the Science Museum in London.

Amy Johnson working on her plane

Survival kit

As well as being able to fix her plane, Amy had to carry her own personal survival kit with her, although there was not much space in her plane.

Amy's kit:		
Flask of tea	Gun	First aid kit
Some boiled sweets	Matches	Several spanners

She also needed to wrap up warm for most of the trip! Every day, she might be flying for eight hours or longer, depending on the winds and the weather.

King George V sent a telegram from Buckingham Palace to the Governor General of Australia, Canberra:

The Queen and I are thankful and delighted to know of Miss Johnson's safe arrival in Australia, and heartily congratulate her upon her wonderful and courageous achievement.

What was life like then?

Very few people flew in the 1920s. Only men were employed as air stewards (or flight attendants) until 1930. Most people travelled by train or boat if they were going to another country, and most of the crew and drivers would have been men. Aeroplanes were still very small – only carrying around 10 to 12 passengers.

What people thought about Amy at the time

Ladies wanted their hair cut just like Amy's, and she was paid to model clothes. The world seemed to have gone Amy Johnson mad!

One of the biggest hit songs of 1930 was 'Amy, Wonderful Amy', performed by Jack Hylton and his orchestra and recorded in June 1930.

Amy was awarded the CBE in 1930 for her achievement. She was certainly an inspirational woman.

Amy appeared in lots of adverts

Amy on the front page of the Illustrated London News, 31 May 1930

What happened next?

Amy continued to fly, and to set records. In 1931, she became the first person to fly direct from London to Moscow in one day. She became the first woman to fly to Japan. In 1932, she set the record for a solo flight to Cape Town, in South Africa. In 1933, along with her husband, she flew from Wales to the USA in record time. In 1934, she started a job for Hillman Airlines, flying passengers every day from London to Paris. She was awarded the Royal Aero Club's Gold Medal in 1936, and was even guest of honour at the opening of the first Butlins Holiday Camp in Skegness.

◄ *1930s photograph of Amy*

When the Second World War started in 1939, she joined the Air Transport Auxiliary, delivering aeroplanes around the country for the RAF. In January 1941, she was delivering a plane to Oxford when she got lost in fog and crashed into the sea off the coast of Kent. No one ever found her body.

Painting of Amy, now in the
National Portrait Gallery, London

Let's think about it!

Have you been on an aeroplane? Share your experiences with a group of friends.

Why was everyone so impressed by this flight by Amy Johnson? Do you think women should be allowed to do everything men can?

Can you find all the countries she visited on a map?

Combined Lower Primary History timeline

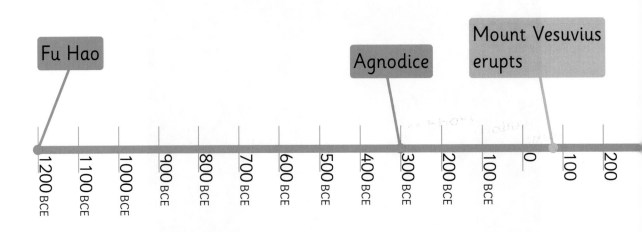

Fu Hao

Agnodice

Mount Vesuvius erupts

1200 BCE | 1100 BCE | 1000 BCE | 900 BCE | 800 BCE | 700 BCE | 600 BCE | 500 BCE | 400 BCE | 300 BCE | 200 BCE | 100 BCE | 0 | 100 | 200

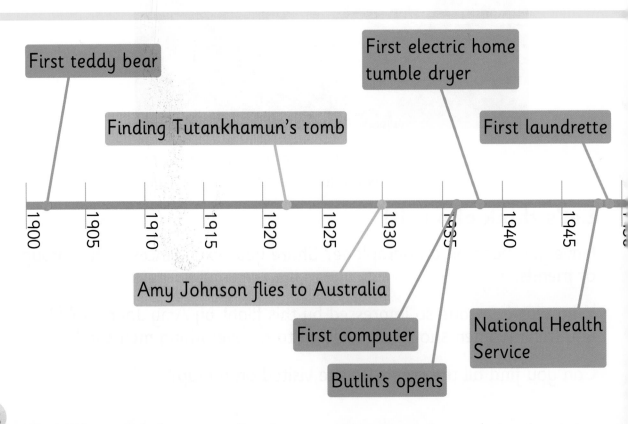

First teddy bear

Finding Tutankhamun's tomb

First electric home tumble dryer

First laundrette

1900 | 1905 | 1910 | 1915 | 1920 | 1925 | 1930 | 1935 | 1940 | 1945

Amy Johnson flies to Australia

First computer

Butlin's opens

National Health Service

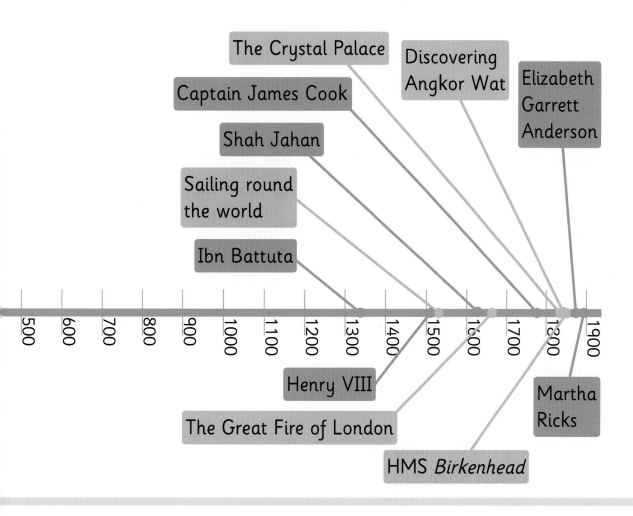

The Crystal Palace

Discovering Angkor Wat

Elizabeth Garrett Anderson

Captain James Cook

Shah Jahan

Sailing round the world

Ibn Battuta

500 600 700 800 900 1000 1100 1200 1300 1400 1500 1600 1700 1800 1900

Henry VIII

The Great Fire of London

HMS *Birkenhead*

Martha Ricks

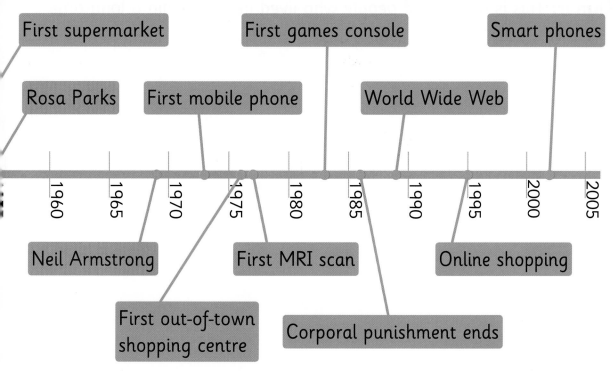

First supermarket

First games console

Smart phones

Rosa Parks

First mobile phone

World Wide Web

1960 1965 1970 1975 1980 1985 1990 1995 2000 2005

Neil Armstrong

First MRI scan

Online shopping

First out-of-town shopping centre

Corporal punishment ends

Glossary

Afterlife: This was where the Ancient Egyptians believed you went when you died.

Cloves: These are the flower buds of a tree grown in Indonesia. They are used in cooking to flavour dishes, or to make things smell nice.

Cockpit: Where the pilot sits in a small plane.

Dense black cloud: Thick, dark cloud which is difficult to see through.

Empire: These are the countries controlled by one other main country.

Erupted: This is when a volcano explodes, throwing out hot gases, stones and lava.

HMS: All ships in the navy had this in their names – it stands for 'His/Her Majesty's Ship'.

Khmer: This is a group of people who lived in Cambodia a long time ago, around 1000 CE. Their language is still spoken by many people in Southeast Asia.

Lava: This is the hot liquid which pours out of the top of a volcano.

Meteorite: A solid piece of rock which has come from outer space.

Nubians: A group of people who lived in southern Egypt.

Pharaoh: An Egyptian ruler.

Pumice stone: This is a volcanic rock, usually light-coloured.

Rigging: These are the ropes, cables and chains supporting the ship's wooden mast, which holds the sails up.

Satellite navigation systems: Help drivers of all kinds of transport find their way around. They use information from space to know where you are.

Solo: When you do something on your own.

Thatch: This is what some roofs are made of – bundles of dried reeds or straw.

20th century: A century is 100 years and the 20th century is the era from 1901 to 2000.

Index

Acknowledgements

The publishers wish to thank the following for permission to reproduce images. Every effort has been made to trace copyright holders and to obtain their permission for the use of copyright materials. The publishers will gladly receive any information enabling them to rectify any error or omission at the first opportunity.

(t = top, c = centre, b = bottom, r = right, l = left)

p4tl and 11 Artexplorer/Alamy Stock Photo; p4tr and 20 Alexey Stiop/Shutterstock; p4bl and 34 Historic Collection/Alamy Stock Photo; p4br and 40 GL Archive/Alamy Stock Photo; p5tl and 23 North Wind Picture Archives/Alamy Stock Photo; p5tr and 56 Granger Historical Picture Archive/Alamy Stock Photo; p5bl and 46b Heritage Image Partnership Ltd/Alamy Stock Photo; p5br and 28 GL Archive/Alamy Stock Photo; p10 Ioana Catalina Echim/Alamy Stock Photo; p13 Photo Resource Hawaii/Alamy Stock Photo; p14 WitR/ Shutterstock; p15 Stock Italia/Alamy Stock Photo; p16 Boyloso/Shutterstock; p17 Old Images/Alamy Stock Photo; p19 Central portico of Angkor Wat, drawing by Therond from a sketch by Mouhot, from Travels in central parts of Indo-China (Siam), Cambodia, and Laos, by the naturalist Henri Mouhot/Veneranda Biblioteca Ambrosiana, Milan, Italy/De Agostini Picture Library/Bridgeman Images; p21 Niday Picture Library/Alamy Stock Photo; p22 IanDagnall Computing/Alamy Stock Photo; p25 Pikoso.kz/Shutterstock; p26 joloei/Shutterstock; p29t The Print Collector/Alamy Stock Photo; p29b Terry Fincher.Photo Int/Alamy Stock Photo; p30 GL Archive/Alamy Stock Photo; p32 PlusONE/Shutterstock; p33 Susie Kearley/Alamy Stock Photo; p35 Michelle Jewell/Shutterstock; p36 The Print Collector/Alamy Stock Photo; p37 The Wreck of HMS Birkenhead off the Cape of Good Hope on 26 Feb. 1852, 1892 (litho) (later colouration), Hemy, Thomas Marie Madawaska (1852-1937)/The Argory, County Armagh, Northern Ireland/Bridgeman Images; p39 David J. Green/Alamy Stock Photo; p41 IanDagnall Computing/Alamy Stock Photo; p42t Hristo Chernev/Alamy Stock Photo; p42b Hristo Chernev/Alamy Stock Photo; p42c Hristo Chernev/Alamy Stock Photo; p43 KGPA Ltd/Alamy Stock Photo; p44 Alexey Fedorenko/Shutterstock; p45l Hristo Chernev/Alamy Stock Photo; p45r Hristo Chernev/Alamy Stock Photo; p47 Petr Bonek/Alamy Stock Photo; p48 Stock Connection Blue/ Alamy Stock Photo; p49 Prashant Kumar/Alamy Stock Photo; p50 Kenneth Garrett/Contributor/Getty Images; p51 UrbanImages/Alamy Stock Photo; p53 Popperfoto/Contributor/Getty Images; p55t Image Courtesy of The Advertising Archives; p55b Chronicle/Alamy Stock Photo; p57 Amy Johnson, c.1930 (oil on canvas), Longstaff, John (1862-1941)/National Portrait Gallery, London, UK/Photo © Stefano Baldini/Bridgeman Images.

We are grateful to the following for permission to reproduce copyright material:

Harvard University Press for the extract on page 11, 'Pliny the Younger, Letters, Volume I: Books 1-7. LCL 55. Translated by Betty Radice. Loeb Classical Library 55. Cambridge, MA: Harvard University Press, 1969.